Help Your Children Succeed in School

A Special Guide for Latino Parents

Mariela Dabbah

SPHINX® PUBLISHING

AN IMPRINT OF SOURCEBOOKS, INC.®
NAPERVILLE, ILLINOIS
www.SphinxLegal.com

First Edition: 2007

Published by: **Sphinx® Publishing, An Imprint of Sourcebooks, Inc.®**

Naperville Office
P.O. Box 4410
Naperville, Illinois 60567-4410
630-961-3900
Fax: 630-961-2168
www.sourcebooks.com
www.SphinxLegal.com

This publication is designed to provide accurate and authoritative information in regard to the subject matter covered. It is sold with the understanding that the publisher is not engaged in rendering legal, accounting, or other professional service. If legal advice or other expert assistance is required, the services of a competent professional person should be sought.

From a Declaration of Principles Jointly Adopted by a Committee of the American Bar Association and a Committee of Publishers and Associations

This product is not a substitute for legal advice.

Disclaimer required by Texas statutes.

Library of Congress Cataloging-in-Publication Data
Dabbah, Mariela.
  Help your children succeed in school / by Mariela Dabbah. -- 1st ed.
    p. cm.
  English-language edition of: Ayude a sus hijos a tener éxito en la escuela.
  ISBN-13: 978-1-57248-614-0 (pbk. : alk. paper)
  ISBN-10: 1-57248-614-7 (pbk. : alk. paper)
  1. Hispanic American children--Education. 2. Hispanic American families. 3. Education--Parent participation--United States. 4. Schools--United States. I. Title.

LC2669.D3513 2006
371.829'68073--dc22
                                                          2006029564

Printed and bound in the United States of America.
VP — 10 9 8 7 6 5 4 3 2 1

Dedication

To my parents Gabriela and Guillermo, for whom the education of their children was always a priority, and to my nieces and nephews: Luciana, Florencia, Martín, Mariano, and Sol

Acknowledgments

This book was possible thanks to the vision of my editor, Dianne Wheeler. I want to thank her for her support in developing this title. To Mike Bowen, my new editor, I owe for the other half of the support.

To Marjorie Venegas and Arturo Poire, I thank you for reviewing the manuscript.

I want to thank the professionals who so kindly shared their views with me: Gerardo Averbuj, Patrick Cortese, John Diamond, Aida Fastag-Carvajal, Felix Flores, María Guasp, Abe Tomás Hughes II, Jodi Pastell, Helen Santiago, Claire Sylvan, Emilio Tenti Fanfani, Marjorie Venegas, and Terry Wisniewski.

I am also grateful to the many parents who shared their concerns and suggestions.

Finally, I would like to particularly thank my friend and colleague Iris Yankelevich not only for sharing her views, but also for her support through the years.

Contents

Introduction

It's a well-known fact that most parents want what is best for their children. Coming from a different country, however, adds a dimension that you should take into consideration when it comes to your children's education. You may think you are doing what is best for them by doing what you used to do in your home country, when many aspects of the system are different in the United States than in Latin America. Being aware of the differences will greatly improve your children's chances of success.

In this book, you will find out how the American school system works, what is expected of you and your children, and what your rights and responsibilities are. You will come away with all the tools you need to help your child not only adapt to the school system, but flourish.

NOTE: Throughout the book I offer Internet addresses where you can find useful information. Keep in mind that sites change often, so if at any point you do not find the information being referenced, just type the name of the organization on **www.google.com** or in any other search engine.

Chapter 1

The Importance of Your Children's Self-Esteem

Entering school for the first time is normally a stressful experience for a child regardless of his or her age. A 4-year-old can be as terrified to enter pre kindergarten as a 9-year-old is to enter third grade. They are both faced with a new situation, new people, a new country, and many times, a new language.

If you have arrived in this country recently, you have to consider your children's own immigration experience. If they were born here or came as infants, have they had the chance to assimilate to the American culture before entering school, or have they only socialized with kids from your home country?

If they were school-age when they came to the U.S., then their situation may be a little harder, as they entered school at a time when most of the other kids have known each other for a few years.

Put yourself in their shoes. Imagine being a young child beginning school with a whole bunch of strangers, with kids and adults who behave differently than what you are used to, and in addition, they speak a language you do not understand. Even though many schools now offer Spanish-speaking teachers and classes, the experience can be quite terrifying nonetheless.

When children begin school for the first time in this country, they may feel a mix of emotions, such as shyness, fear, and embarrassment. It is important that you help them through this process by showing your support and your love. It is a critical moment in their lives, one when they will decide—even if subconsciously—whether school is a positive experience or not. If they have a high self-esteem, they will endure this transition and quickly learn to adapt to the system, like many children do. On the other hand, if their self-esteem is low, they can become discouraged by their classmate's jokes, or by a sense of not fitting in and not belonging to the school community. This is what you want to avoid at all costs, as it is one of the main reasons children drop out of school. (See Chapter 11 for more information about helping your children stay in school.)

What can you do to help your children feel part of the group? The following is a list of important things you should consider.

- Find out if the school offers sports that your children used to play back home, such as soccer, and enroll them immediately.

- Participate in as many parents' activities right from the beginning, so the children feel that school is a good place to be involved.

■   Invite your children's friends to your house to play.
    Help them develop a group of friends as quickly as
    possible. Allow your children to connect with chil-
    dren of other cultures.

Cultural Tip

Many large U.S. cities are much more multicultural than your native country. Avoid making racial
or cultural comments about other kids or teachers.
Be careful with comments you make about people
on television or people you deal with in your daily
life. When kids are young they easily absorb these
stereotypes, which may eventually interfere with
their relationships at school.

Chapter 2

How Your Personal Experience Affects Your Approach To Education

Given that parents are the most influential people in children's lives, everything you do (or do not do) affects them. It's very important to be aware of how your current situation or your past experiences may affect the way in which you view and approach your children's education.

Patrick Cortese and Terry Wisniewski from New Learning Concepts, an educational book publisher, suggest that you become inculturated. (In other words, that you learn the culture of your local school system in order to get the best results for your child.) The way it was back home or when you went to school is not how it is in the United States. You must be able to shift your thinking into that of a parent with children in American schools, where the expectation is that you will participate in and support your children's education as much as possible.

You are in the U.S. now, and you need to learn what to expect of the system here, as well as what it expects of you and your child. If you do not understand how the system works in the U.S., your children will not do as well as they could.

The following sections look at some common beliefs that many Latino parents have regarding their children's education and the school system in the U.S. You will see that there are some drastic differences from what you may be used to, and that you must respond differently to your children's teachers and the school than you would back home.

Belief #1—School is Better in the U.S. than in Latin America

Many of you grew up believing that education in the U.S. was superior to that in your own countries. You may have known youngsters who left your country to study in the United States.

FACT: *In the United States, there is a wide range of performance levels throughout the country. Your job is to explore the schools in your area and find one that suits your values and your educational goals for your children.*

Belief #2—Teachers are Revered

In your country, school teachers may be revered as important and respected professionals. Nobody questions their knowledge or their ability to teach children. Nobody questions the school as an institution. Children attend school and parents' involvement is limited.

FACT: *In the United States, teachers are often considered underpaid and not given much respect. There is a wide range in the education and experience of teachers, resulting in good teachers and bad teachers. Plus, every public school is different. There are good schools, which have more funding and equipment, and there are the not-so-good schools, which may be lacking critical, basic tools for a modern education. You need to ask questions to find the best school for your child and to make sure your child is learning.*

Belief #3—The School is Always Right

In many Latin American countries, the school is a higher authority than the parents. Because of this belief, parents seldom question this authority and may take a step back and not get involved with the school, as getting involved may be seen as disrespectful towards educators.

FACT: *In the United States, your authority is always above the school's authority. You are the person who will always make the decisions on your children's behalf. If the school is doing something you do not agree with, you have every right to demand that it stops. You also have the right to find out why something is taking place. However, to be involved, you have to express your position. In addition, you may need to take action in your children's behalf.*

Belief #4—Undocumented Aliens Cannot be Involved in the School System

If you are undocumented, you probably fear most government institutions and authorities. This probably includes your children's school. This fear keeps you from visiting your children's school and being a part of their learning experience.

FACT: *In the United States, your children have the right to learn even if their family is undocumented. Nobody in the school system can ask about your immigration status, so the school is a very safe place for you and your children. It is also a place where you can meet other people who may be in a similar position, and others who can help you and your children with questions and problems.*

Belief #5—Your Children are Already Doing Better than You, So There is no Need for More Education

You may think your children are doing so much better than you did in your country that you are just happy they are attending high school. You may have no expectations for your children to go to college, or may believe that they do not need to go in order to find a good paying job.

FACT: *In the United States, a high school diploma will only enable your children to work in very menial jobs. In order for your children to do better economically and move up socially, they need to go to college. According to the U.S.Census Bureau, a high school graduate makes an average salary of $25,191 while a person with a Bachelor's degree makes an average of $41,287. Part of your job in helping your children succeed is to pick the right high school for them to attend and to work with the school and teachers so that your children can get the most out of their education. A lower percentage of students who graduate from public high schools go to college than those who graduate from a private school, so helping them choose the right high school is an even larger responsibility.*

Belief #6—Only English Speakers Can be Involved in Their Children's Education

You do not speak English, therefore you believe you cannot attend parent/teacher conferences, express your wishes and expectations, or otherwise be involved in your children's school.

FACT: *In most U.S. schools there are people who speak Spanish—it might be a guidance counselor, a teacher, a secretary, or another parent. Ask the school to send you communications in Spanish. The school will provide translation services, so you can ask for an interpreter to be present at parent/teacher conferences. If you do not get involved, the school might interpret your absence as a lack of interest in your children's education and progress, and not because of a perceived language barrier issue. Not being able to speak the same language may cause some frustration and extra effort on everyone's part, but it should not prevent you from you being involved in your children's education.*

Belief #7—The School's Values are the Same as Yours

In your country, school is a place where teachers—who are part of the community—take care of your children just as you would. For example, if the children misbehave, they gets disciplined.

FACT: *In the United States, children's discipline is handled differently, and the school often requires that the parents get involved when there is an issue at school. If the school does exercise certain types of corporal punishments (like smacking with a ruler), as the parent, you have the authority to instruct the school not to administer certain types of physical punishment. In any event, the school will never discipline the children the way you do.*

Belief #8—The School System is Intimidating

Maybe you did not go to school yourself, so you feel threatened by it. Maybe you have tried to be involved with your children's school, but a teacher or principal made you feel uncomfortable for whatever reason. That fear is preventing you from being involved with your children's teachers and their school.

FACT: *In the United States, schools try to be very parent-friendly. If your child attends a school that is not, you should consider asking for a school change. Do not be afraid and make an effort to get involved. Otherwise, your children will get the idea that school is not important and they will not do as well as they could.*

Belief #9—Taking My Children Out of School for Extended Periods of Time is Not a Problem

You work very hard and miss your family back home. It is common to take your children on long trips that begin before school is out or end after school has began.

FACT: *In the United States, school attendance is very important, and it will determine whether your child passes a class or even the year. When you take your children out of school for trips, vacations, or to help you at work, you are hurting their education. You are also sending them two* *poor messages: 1) that they can take their responsibilities lightly and 2) that school is not important.*

Cultural Tip

There is always a delicate balance between assimilating to a new system and keeping your cultural heritage alive. When it comes to formal education, however, you need to learn how the American system works so that your children have the best chance to succeed in this country. Education is the key that will open many, many doors for them. It is to your benefit and theirs to adapt as soon as possible. Learn how the system works and help your children through the process. You will see the rewards for years to come!

Chapter 3
The Basics

American schools are part of a very complex educational system that many Americans have trouble understanding. Learning the intricacies will help you feel at ease with the different requirements and regulations. In this chapter, you will find a clear explanation of the various programs available, the logistics involved with sending your children to school (enrolling age, initial placement, transportation, school calendar, supplies, etc.), your rights related to your immigration status, and breakfast and lunch programs.

I suggest that you read this section carefully, as it will answer most of your initial questions about how schools work in the United States.

Enrolling Age
Every child age 5 to 21 has the right to attend public school until he or she graduates from high school. Children of school-age cannot be turned down because of age or limited prior education.

Children begin kindergarten the year they turn five. In most states, there are some available seats for prekindergarten, but there are usually not enough for all the 4-year-olds who want to attend. Find out what is the procedure in your district to get a seat in a prekindergarten class. In some states, you may be placed on a waiting list when your child turns three. Usually, enrolling your child implies going to the school with several pieces of information. You can find all the details about the documents needed to enroll your child in Chapter 4.

Immigration Status

Children have a right to attend school regardless of their immigration status or the status of their parents. No one may ask for the immigration status of the child or of his or her family. Even though some schools may ask for a Social Security number, it is usually just for administrative purposes and you are not required to give this information. Your children are entitled to receive all school services, such as textbooks, breakfast, lunch, and transportation. Although there is usually a fee involved for these services (like book rental, meals, and transportation), your child may receive them for free if you qualify. Again, you will find more details in Chapter 4.

Initial Placement

A student is usually placed in a grade according to his or her previous school record. If he or she does not have one, he or she will usually be placed in a grade appropriate to his or her age. The school will then contact former schools to obtain the student's records.

If there are no existing records or they cannot be obtained because they are located in another country, the school will evaluate the child according to procedures that vary from district to district. According to this evaluation, the school may recommend that your child receive special services, such as a dual language program, special education, or a gifted and talented program.

Bilingual Programs and English as a Second Language

When a child enters the school system, the parents usually have to complete a survey regarding the child's home language. If your answers show that your children may not be fluent in English, they will be tested. Students who score below a certain percentage are required to take either bilingual education or English as a Second Language (ESL). The children will be tested every year so the school may follow their progress.

According to the No Child Left Behind Act (NCLB), a law passed by the Bush Administration in 2002, schools have to inform parents if their child needs bilingual or ESL education. Parents have the right to an explanation of the different program options and to an orientation session on program requirements, state standards, and assessments. It is very important that you attend these sessions both so that you understand the programs your children will be in, and so that you can keep track of their progress.

There are several models of bilingual education, and sometimes, if the district is large enough, you can choose the one that you think will benefit your child the most. Other times there is only one program available, and it is generally one of the following.

- Transitional programs. The goal is to transition the child into English as quickly as possible, with significant instruction given in English.

- Maintenance bilingual education. The goal is to develop academic proficiency in Spanish while the child learns vocabulary in English. Each year the English portion of instruction increases.

- Dual language programs. Students with limited English proficiency (who speak Spanish) and native English speakers (who don't speak Spanish) work together in the same class with the goal of developing proficiency in both languages.

- English as a Second Language. Students learn to speak, write, and read English from a teacher trained to teach second language learners.

Cultural Tip

As an adult, you may think that you do not need to speak English because everyone around you speaks Spanish. Although it is true that in many communities you could survive with Spanish as your only language, in order to progress and succeed in the U.S. market, you need to speak, read, and write English correctly. Find out about free ESL courses for adults at a public library, community college, high school, or local nonprofit organizations. There are also many videos and CDs you can borrow from the library. (Watching soap operas in English is another way to learn the language.)

Special Education

If your child needs special services, the school is required to provide them. Since these services cost the school a lot of money, it will document the ways in which it tried to help the student through regular education services before considering special education. It is reasonable for the school to try and keep the child in regular classes until a formal determination has been made that special services are required.

If the school personnel suspect that a child has a disability, they can refer him or her for a special education evaluation. In general, a child cannot be evaluated for special education without the parent's consent. However, in some cases, school personnel document events and create a file that can then be used for a special hearing, where the evidence is presented to an

> Helen Santiago, former New York
> City Schools District Superintendent
> and current Executive Director of
> the New York Education Initiative at
> the College Board, suggests that you
> do not allow your children to be
> tested for special education the first
> year they are in school. Although, in
> general, district evaluators will
> refrain from testing a newly arrived
> child, there are some schools that
> tend to erroneously think that
> when children don't speak English
> well, they need to be placed in
> special education.

impartial officer. Officers can then order an evaluation if it is in the best interest of the child.

If you believe that your child has a disability, you can also request an evaluation. Make your request in writing, and do so as soon as you believe your child needs extra assistance. If your child is entering a new school, and he or she has received special assistance at his or her previous school, talk to the school about what services they provide and what you need to do in order to make sure that your child receives the services he or she needs right from the start.

Some districts offer bilingual special education classes to accommodate immigrant children's needs.

Transportation

According to how close you live from the school, your child will be offered either free yellow bus transportation, or discounted or free public transportation fares. Find out at the time of enrollment which of these options you qualify for. If your child needs to take a bus, request the bus schedule and ask about the bus stop where your child will get on and be dropped off. Also, it is very important to become acquainted with the driver. This is the person who will be responsible for getting your child to and from school every day.

Books

Unlike in most Latin American countries, public schools in the U.S. supply all the textbooks that children need for their school work, so you do not have to worry about buying them yourself. Although there are usually fees involved in renting these textbooks and for other activities, such as lab use or for special events, you may receive these services for free or at a reduced price if you qualify for a free or reduced lunch program. Talk to the principal when you enroll your children.

The school will have a library in which your children can check out books, but it is always a good idea to get a library card from your local public library. Your children will have reports and other homework that may require using the resources offered at a public library. Plus, many libraries have computers that your children can use to access the Internet or help prepare their homework.

Breakfast and Lunch

Most schools participate in the National School Food Programs, a federal program that provides funding for free and reduced-price breakfast and lunch to children who qualify. The school will send you a form at the beginning of the year to assess your eligibility according to your income. Children from families with incomes below 130% of the poverty level are eligible for free meals. Those between 130% and 185% are eligible for reduced-price meals. Those households with incomes over 185% of the poverty level pay full price.

If you want to check what your family is eligible for, go to **www.fns.usda.gov** and click on "National School

Lunch Program," and then "Income Eligibility Guidelines." On this website you can also find the chart that gives you the different income levels per household size. For example, if there are four people in your household, you need to base your calculations on an income of $34,873. If you make less than $45,334.90 (130% of the $34,873), your children will qualify to receive free meals. If you make between $45,334.90 and $64,515.05 (130% to 185% of $34,873), your children will qualify for reduced meals.

Keep in mind that you do not need to be a legal immigrant to be eligible.

Dress Code

Many private and parochial schools have required uniforms for years. Today, more and more public schools are opting for uniforms. They have observed that implementing a policy for uniforms has many of the following benefits:

- decrease violence and theft—even life-threatening situations—among students over designer clothing or expensive sneakers;

- help prevent gang members from wearing gang colors and insignia at school;

- instill discipline in students;

- help parents and students resist peer pressure;

- help students concentrate on their schoolwork; and,

- help school officials recognize intruders who come to the school.

While some schools have a mandatory uniform policy, others only have a voluntary one. Schools with a mandatory policy usually have an opt-out option, which means that students can opt out of the uniform requirement with parent consent.

In many cases, school uniforms are less expensive than the clothing that students typically wear to school. Nonetheless, the cost of purchasing a uniform may be a burden to some families. That is the reason why many schools have programs to assist parents. They may provide free uniforms, refer you to community organizations that supply them, organize fund raisers to buy uniforms for people who can not afford them, and so on. To find out what your school offers, talk to the principal in your school.

Schools with no uniform requirement may still implement a dress code. This is usually done to encourage a safer environment, for example, by forbidding clothes with certain language or gang colors.

Whatever your school's uniform and dress code policy, parental involvement is very important to make your children comply with this requirement. You need to make sure the uniform is washed or cleaned over the weekend and ready to wear the next week. If your school does not require a uniform, instill in your children a need to go to school clean and neatly dressed.

School Calendar

Every school publishes a monthly calendar of activities. In this calendar you will see test dates, holidays, half days, parent/teacher conferences, and special activities, such as festivals, fund raisers, and book fairs.

Many times the calendar is posted on the school's website, but it almost always gets sent home with the students. Review it and then post it on your refrigerator to keep up to date with your children's schedules.

Chapter 4

Tackling One Issue at a Time

If you have recently arrived in the United States or if this is your first encounter with the education system here, you are probably at a loss. If you and your child do not speak English, the feeling of being lost may be even more overwhelming. You may feel like you do not know who to talk to or where to go.

Understanding the framework of the schools is an important step in understanding the entire system. Although each state has its own laws, most of them require that children begin school by age 6 or 7. However, schools group children in various ways.

Elementary School (Primary School)

For some districts, elementary school covers grades kindergarten–5, for others grades kindergarten–6, and still for others kindergarten–8. Children begin kindergarten when they are 5 years old. As mentioned earlier, there are some free prekindergarten placements available, but not enough for all the 4-year-olds who wish to enroll. (Check your local school for more details.)

Middle School

Middle school generally includes grades 6 through 8. Children are usually between the ages of 11 and 13. This is a tough age for your children, as it is usually when puberty develops in full force. You may see your children starting to pull away from you, so it is important that you stay in even greater contact with the school and your children's teachers to make sure you know what is going on in your children's lives and education.

Some middle schools are called junior high school and cover grades 7–9.

High School

In general, grades 9 through 12 are considered high school, and children range from 14 to 17. Grade 9 is also called freshman year; grade 10 is called sophomore year; grade 11 is called junior year; and, grade 12 is called senior year. As discussed later in the book, you may think that your children are older now, so you don't need to be involved as much. That would be a big mistake. Teenagers are very vulnerable, and it is a key time for you to remain involved in their education.

District Office

In each neighborhood, schools are grouped under one school district. There is usually a district office where you will find the administration that oversees several schools, from elementary to high school. In large cities, districts may encompass anywhere from ten to one hundred schools or more. In smaller suburban or rural areas, a school district may only have one K–12 (kindergarten through grade 12) school.

At the district office level, you will find the superintendent of schools (the person in charge of the entire system) and the directors of all the main curricular areas, such as math, reading, science, social studies, and ESL. Some school systems are centralized, which means that most of the decisions are made at the district level. Others are decentralized, which means that most of the decisions are made at the school level.

Individual Schools

At each school you will find the principal (the director of the school), and depending on the size of the school, you may find one or more assistant principals. You may also find coordinators for the different programs. For example, science coordinator, ESL coordinator, or parent coordinator. In addition, schools usually have a psychologist or a social worker, a nurse, and a librarian.

Looking at the Different Types of Schools

In the United States, children attend the public school that is closest to their home. Therefore, it is very important that you explore what the schools are like in an area before you settle down. Different states, towns, and even neighborhoods offer very different levels of education. It is important to ask questions to find out what the schools are like in your area, because you may be able to provide your children with a better education by moving a few minutes away.

As you will read throughout this book, one of the keys to helping your children succeed in school is to ask questions. While in your country you might enroll your children in the school closest to your house (or maybe the only school near your house), here you need to look at the options first. Different schools will lead to different opportunities for your children's futures.

Public Schools

Public schools are funded with state, local, and federal funds, and they are free. States and school districts differ in the tax rates they approve and in the budget choices they make. That is why each school district has a different amount of money to spend, and consequently, different class sizes, facilities, and quality of teachers.

Urban and Suburban Public Schools

Schools located in an urban area usually have a more diverse student population. The children come from a variety of socioeconomic, cultural, and linguistic backgrounds. Although classes tend to be larger and funds more limited, it is easier to find bilingual and ESL classes in these schools. Also, some urban school districts are large enough to offer schools with a special orientation, such as arts, drama, or science.

The suburban public schools are usually better funded and tend to have a larger percentage of college-bound students. Many of them offer a wide variety of programs, such as sports (soccer, swimming, baseball, etc.), music and drama, foreign languages, and special clubs (debate club, film club, chess club, etc.). Again, this will vary from one town to the next, so you need to do some research before you decide to settle in any given area.

Private Schools

Private schools operate on tuition income, donations, and funds from organizations. They charge different amounts, depending on the school.

There are many types of private schools, from religious schools to schools that specialize in a specific area like science or the arts. There are also schools that emphasize creative learning or student-directed learning.

What you have to remember, however, is that the quality of these schools also varies widely, so you need to ask a lot of questions before you make the decision to enroll your child in a private school.

Catholic School

Many Latino parents decide to send their children to Catholic schools, not only because they have a good reputation and are usually less expensive than other private schools, but also because they promote values that are relevant to the Latino culture. Just as with other schools, you should conduct thorough research before enrolling your children, because not all Catholic schools are equal. If you would like to send your children to Catholic school and you cannot afford to pay for their education, you may want to contact the

Archdiocese of your area. They may have a Catholic Education Foundation that can provide you with financial aid.

You can search the American School Directory online at **www.asd.com** if you subscribe for a small fee (you will probably only need a month subscription to do the research). This website allows you to gather relevant information on 105,000 K–12 public, private, and Catholic schools.

Charter Schools

A charter school is a nonsectarian public school that operates without many of the regulations that apply to traditional public schools. The charter establishing each such school is a performance contract detailing the school's mission, program, goals, students served, methods of assessment, and ways to measure success. The charters are usually granted for three to five years. At the end of the term, the entity granting the charter may renew the school's contract. Charter schools are accountable to their sponsor—usually a state or local school board—to produce positive academic results and adhere to the charter contract. The basic idea behind charter schools is that they have increased autonomy in return for this accountability.

Most charter schools intend to:

- increase opportunities for learning and access to quality education for all students;

- create choice for parents and students within the public school system;

- encourage innovative teaching practices; and,

- encourage community and parent involvement in public education.

Anyone can attend a charter school. In some states, however, these schools serve a greater number of minorities or economically disadvantaged students than traditional public schools.

Charter schools do not charge tuition and they are funded by the government according to enrollment. As of 2004, forty states had passed charter laws. In the school year 2004–05, there were more than 3,000 charter schools operating nationwide.

The Center for Education Reform (**www.edreform.com**) publishes the "National Charter School Directory," which provides contact information and profiles of charter schools in operation across the country. It also provides information on specially-focused schools, such as Arts-Based, Core Knowledge, Latino Culture, and Montessori schools. To find a charter school in your area, visit the U.S. Charter Schools website at **www.uscharterschools.org**.

Identify the School for Your Child

The first thing to do when choosing a school for your children is to identify where the public school they would attend is located. Start talking to your neighbors, the librarian at the local public library, or local merchants to identify the school that is closest to your home. Try to find out the school district's address and visit the district to obtain information about which school your child should attend, what the enrollment procedures are, and what programs they offer at that school.

If school is in session, visit the school assigned to your children and make sure they will feel comfortable there. Find out if the school has the programs your children need, whether it is arts, science, special education, or anything else. Get a sense for the school environment. Will your children fit in? Will they feel like a part of the school community?

Also, find out from the district office the math, reading, and science scores of the different schools, what percentage of high school students graduate, and what percentage of students go to college from that district.

Although it is true that you will most likely need to send your child to the school closest to your home, or the one the district assigns to you, it is important to do a little research. Many times, there are magnet elementary, middle, or high schools that any child from the district can attend. These magnet schools are designed around a theme. For example, there are multicultural magnet schools, science and technology magnet schools, law and government magnet schools, and so on. You can also visit Magnet Schools of America at **www.magnet.edu/objectives.htm**.

If you realize that the school your child was assigned to by the district is not appropriate, you may ask for another school that has programs that suit your child. If you don't like any of the schools in a school district, you may need to consider moving to an area that has better schools.

Keep in mind that if your child's school is identified as in need of improvement by the NCLB Act, your child may be eligible to request a transfer to another school in the district. (However, given the stress that the good schools in any given district bear by receiving so many transfers, many school districts are beginning to limit the number of transfers they allow per year.)

However, the NCLB Act places a lot of emphasis on choices. To learn more about what your child may be entitled to under this law, you can visit the website **www.ed.gov/nclb**, and click on "Recursos en español." Then, click on the subject or theme your child is most interested in, and you can then search for schools in your area.

Cultural Tip

Sometimes it is hard for Latinos to speak up and ask for more than they are offered. So, when a school district assigns your children seats in a given school, you might be grateful and go away without further research. Remember that the more research you do, the better their chances to get into a good school with good programs.

Most school districts have websites. Visit the websites and compare schools within the district. Then, visit the individual schools' websites to find out about the special activities and programs they offer. You can visit **www.greatschools.net** to get a lot of information about schools in each state. You can get test scores, student-to-teacher ratio, parents' comments, ethnic make-up of the school, and much more. You can even see a comparison among all the schools in the same school district.

Identify a Contact Person

Once you choose your children's school, it is critical that you identify who will be your contact person. It has to be someone you can call any time you need to receive or provide information to the school. If you do not speak English, you obviously need to find someone who speaks Spanish. It could be the guidance counselor, school psychologist, a teacher, the ESL coordinator, an administrator, the principal, or an assistant principal. Make sure you get that person's name and phone number both at school and at home. Do not forget to give them your information, as well.

Understanding the Enrollment Procedure

After finding the school best suited for your children, you will have to go through the enrollment procedure. It is not a difficult process, just one that needs to be done so the school can set up all the necessary paperwork for your children. To enroll your children, you will need to bring the following:

- photo identification, like a driver's license or passport (you do not need a visa);

- a birth certificate;

- Social Security number (some schools request it, but children cannot be denied enrollment because they, or you, do not have one);

- proof of residency, which is just proof of where you live (and has nothing to do with proof of immigration status), such as a letter from your landlord or a utility bill (telephone or electricity) from the month previous to enrollment;

- the children's report cards from the school in your country of origin (if the child is new to the American school system), translated, so you don't run the risk of your child being enrolled in a lower grade because he or she does not speak English; and,

- vaccination records, also translated. If you do not have the records and you cannot get them, the child will have to be revaccinated, which can usually be done at a community health center. Ask the school which vaccines they require. The common ones include:

  - diphtheria;

  - pertussis (whooping cough—for children through age 6);

  - tetanus;

  - polio;

  - rubeola (measles);

  - rubella (3 day measles);

  - mumps;

- varicella (chicken pox); and,

- hepatitis B.

Also, schools usually require a physical and dental examination for children entering the system for the first time, and sometimes at certain other intervals (such as before entering 5th and 9th grades).

However, having the right paperwork is only half of the battle. You need to follow the strict time line that schools follow for enrollment—and everything else, for that matter.

Cultural Tip

Latinos have a different concept of time than Americans. It is not better or worse, it just does not work in this country as well as it does in Latin America. So, keep in mind that when people here give you a deadline, they mean it. There are no extensions or exceptions and you can lose spots for your children if you do not fill out the information or file the papers by the time you are told. The same is true about dates for tests, appointments to see the teacher or principal, vacation days, and school days. Children can lose the school year if they are absent more than a certain number of days. Find out the maximum number of absences they can have when you enroll them.

Extracurricular Activities

Most schools offer a number of extracurricular activities. Whether it is a foreign language club, arts, science competitions, or anything else, you should find out, at the time of enrollment, how your children can participate in these exciting activities and if there is any cost involved. These activities will help your children further develop their self-esteem, while socializing with other children, learning responsibility, and gaining a host of other important values. Being involved with other children is an important part of the process of assimilation. Your children will be in close contact with the American culture and values, and will absorb them in a very spontaneous way.

Chapter 5

Standards-Based Education

Following the NCLB Act, school districts across the country are implementing standards-based education. This is a process for planning, delivering, monitoring, and improving academic programs. In standards-based education, students learn what is important, rather than allowing textbooks to dictate what they should learn. It aims for a deep level of student understanding that goes beyond traditional textbook instruction.

Standards-based provides clear expectations for all students. Teachers know what they are expected to teach and students know what they are expected to learn. Under this system, parents also know what the expectations are for everyone involved.

The Curriculum

The NCLB mandates that all states create strong standards that specify what each child should know and learn in grades 3 through 8. You can find important information in Spanish about this law and about the

White House Initiative on Educational Excellence for Hispanic Americans at **www.yosipuedo.gov/wwa/ index.html**.

Unfortunately, a book such as this cannot include the details of what your children should learn in each grade, because each school system across the country has a different curriculum. However, you can visit your school's or district's website to find out the curriculum of a particular school. Most of them have a Web page where you can see what students are supposed to know by the end of each grade.

If your children's school or school district does not offer this service, you can visit Mid-Continent Research for Education and Learning's website at **www.mcrel.org/standards-benchmarks/docs/ factsheet.asp**. Click on "Content Knowledge: A Compendium of Standards and Benchmarks for K-12 Education," and then on the "searchable database online." You can search the database by subject area and then by grade level. You can also find videos in Spanish about the standards when you go to **www.nationaldialogue.org/resources/resource.htm**.

You can also visit the websites of other schools for some guidance on what children are supposed to learn in each grade level. Knowing what your children should learn will enable you to follow their progress and will alert you if the school is not teaching according to the outcome expected. The following are some websites you can check for guidance.

- www.sarasota.k12.fl.us/StudentSkills (Sarasota, Florida)

- www.nycenet.edu/Offices/TeachLearn (New York City, New York)

You may want to visit the Core Knowledge website. The Spanish resource area can be found at **www.coreknowledge.org/CK/resrcs/Spanish**. This organization believes that there should be one common curriculum for the entire country. They offer an online Spanish edition of their books about what your children need to know for each grade, from kindergarten to third grade.

Also, check Family Education Network, part of Pearson Education (a large education publisher) at **www.familyeducation.com**. You will find information on what your children are expected to learn in each grade, and much more.

Once you know what your children are supposed to learn in each grade, you can verify that they are actually learning it, and if you realize that they are not, you may want to talk to their teachers about it.

<u>Cultural Tip</u>

You may think that because your children have been promoted to the next grade, they have learned what they were supposed to learn. However, in the United States, many schools will promote a child even if he or she has not learned what he or she was supposed to. This is called social promotion, and the basis for it is that retention affects students' attitude, behavior, and attendance. That is why it is so important that you remain alert when it comes to your children's achievements, and you don't assume that because they "passed," everything is okay.

Standardized Tests

Standardized tests are designed to give a common measure of students' performance. Because large numbers of students throughout the country take the same test, they give educators a common standard of measure. Educators use these standardized tests to determine how well school programs are succeeding, or to get an idea of the skills and abilities of their students.

Some popular tests include the California Achievement Tests (CAT), the Stanford Achievement Test (SAT), the Iowa Test of Basic Skills (ITBS), and the Stanford-Binet Intelligence Scale.

In What Grades are Tests Taken?

There is a federal test called National Assessment of Education Progress (NAEP), which tracks the national progress of students in 4th, 8th, and 10th grade to see how well the different states are doing in math and reading. This test is administered to a random sampling of students in each district.

Following the NCLB Act, children from 3rd to 8th grade have to be tested. However, each city and state decides which one of the standardized test to administer and when.

If your children are English Language Learners, they might be exempt from taking it. Make sure you talk to the teacher and principal about this.

Helping Your Children Succeed on a Standardized Test

In order to help your children succeed at a standardized test, there are a few things you can do. You can get involved in the process, finding out as much as possible about the test; help your children practice by getting them practice tests; inquiring about your children's eligibility for additional testing time; incorporating some of the testing behaviors into your daily life; and, practicing certain skills.

Know as Much about the Test as Possible

Most tests are organized around curriculum areas. In the lower grades, these areas are math, language arts, and reading. In the upper grades, they are science, math, language arts, reading, and, occasionally, social studies, or American and/or state history. To find out the content of the tests, contact your children's teachers, your district office, or your state department of education.

Ask for Practice Tests

There are many books that feature practice tests. You can find them at libraries and bookstores. These are usually past test, so they are actual examples of the test. The school can also provide you with other exercises to prepare your children.

Find out if Your Children Qualify for Special Test-Taking Accommodations

If your children have been identified for special services or have learning disabilities, they may be exempt from the test or may be able to take it under special conditions, such as in a different room or for a longer amount of time. Ask the principal or school psychologist.

Incorporate Test-Taking Behaviors into Everyday Homework Activities

Most standardized tests are timed, encourage children to skip items they do not know and come back to them later, and rely on students understanding directions. To practice these behaviors, encourage your children to skip items they do not know when doing homework and come back to them later. Also, time certain homework activities. Finally, ask your children to read the directions of the homework and explain them to you, to make sure they understand the directions.

You can also practice these behaviors with everyday activities. For instance, ask your children to read the directions for a recipe or directions to put together a toy or a household tool, and to explain them to you in their own words. Depending on the children's ages, you may also time activities, such as cleaning up their rooms, preparing breakfast, or running an errand.

Practice Skills at Home

Besides practicing taking the different tests with past copies of the tests themselves, you may want to help your children develop the skills being tested. Since tests are organized around curriculum areas, the following are some ideas you can implement to prepare for each one of them.

■ Reading—Most reading exams test comprehension skills; try to assess your childrens' ability to understand what they read and make inferences; and, test their ability to predict where the story is going and their ability to extract information from the story they read.

   In order to develop these skills, you should engage your children whenever they are reading. Ask them to explain the plot, the story's characters, and the setting. You can even practice this when watching a television show or a movie. The idea is to have your children pull out information from the story. If you read a book together, ask questions about what happened and why they think things happened that way.

- Writing—Standardized tests usually have a writing section where children are given a writing prompt, which is just an idea to get them to write. The point is to assess your children's ability to develop an idea and present it logically in writing.

  You can help them practice this skill by giving them projects like "Write a letter to the town suggesting that they put a new traffic light in a dangerous intersection" or "Write instructions to tape a program from the TV."

- Language Arts—Tests in this curriculum area focus on your children's use of language. So, it is important to help them improve their vocabulary. Have your children look up difficult everyday words in the dictionary. Ask them to find synonyms (different words that mean the same) and antonyms (words that mean the opposite). Ask your children to alphabetize things around the house, like books, CDs, and movies.

- Math—Depending on your children's grade levels, the math test will try to assess specific skills. You will have to adapt your activities to what they are supposed to be learning at their particular grade. Taking that into consideration, you can encourage your children to learn to count by two's, three's, and five's. Create graphs based on family activities and practice reading graphs together. For example, develop a graph for each person's responsibilities and who they should report to. Teach your children how to tell time and practice it with them. Ask them to keep track of time, or to design their day hour by hour. Talk about money, making change, how much things cost.

Regardless of the subject area, you may want to ask the teachers what additional suggestions they have for activities at home.

Help Your Children be Ready for the Test

On the days prior to the test, try to engage in relaxing activities that will reduce your children's anxiety. Because some tests can go on for a few days, build in some time for fun and physical activities during this period.

Make sure your children rest the night before the test. A good night's sleep is crucial for a good performance, as is eating a good, nutritious breakfast. This is a key meal to increase your children's mental readiness. Research has shown that eating the right foods in the morning may increase neuron connections, therefore improving mental activity, such as the use of memory and other mental functions. The best way to accomplish this is by eating foods that provide energy, such as whole grain cereals and fruits. The morning is also a great time to feed your children proteins, such as eggs, milk, and yogurt. You can offer them natural juices like orange, apple, tomato, or carrot, but you should avoid giving them sweetened juices or colas. Anything that contains sugar or white carbohydrates (such as white bread or sugary cereals) should be avoided, as these items will give your children a rush of energy that will drop very quickly, making them feel tired and hungry.

For test day, you should also pack some nutritious snacks for in-between test times. These can include nuts (like almonds or peanuts), raisins, a cheese or peanut butter sandwich made with whole wheat bread, or a piece of fruit.

Susan Landon, the mother of a 9-year-old who is in 4th grade, says that she does not worry so much about scores yet, but she does make sure her daughter studies for a test and expects her to perform well. "The day before yesterday, she forgot to bring her book home from school, so yesterday we studied until 10:30 p.m. and this morning I woke her up at 6:30 a.m. so she could continue studying."

Find out the Meaning of the Test

One important thing that you want to know regarding these tests is how the scores will be used directly regarding your children. They may have no impact and only be a gauge for school group scores, or they may be a direct evaluation of your children. Find out from the school answers to the following questions.

- What will happen if your children do exceptionally well?

- Will they be placed in a gifted program?

- What if they do not receive a high enough score?

- Will they be held back or receive special tutoring?

Find out this information before the test to better help your children prepare.

Cultural Tip

Perhaps in your country of origin, when your children in elementary or middle school take a test, you do not worry too much. You may think "it's just a test." In the United States, however, schoolwork and school tests are taken seriously. Parents who want their kids to have successful educational careers try to participate as much as possible from very early on. Test-taking skills and good performance are looked upon as important life-long skills. Not only will they be useful throughout high school and then in college, but the competition to enter the best colleges starts with good scores at the middle-school level or even earlier, depending on the school district.

Other Means of Grading Your Children: Class Participation and Portfolio Assessment

You need to be aware that testing is not the only way in which your children will be evaluated. Their participation in class is crucial to their overall grades. It is good for you to frequently ask your children—and their teachers—if they participate in class. If they do not, you need to address the reason with your children. What is keeping them from raising his hand? Are they overly shy? Afraid to fail? Do they not know the answers? Once you find out what is keeping them from actively participating in class you may want to discuss it with the teacher to find suitable solutions.

Also, in the last few years, a new way of assessing students has made its way into the classroom. It is called portfolio assessment, and it is usually used in the areas of reading, writing, and foreign language. Generally speaking, a literacy portfolio, for example, is a systematic collection of a several teacher observations and student products collected over time that reflect a student's developmental status and progress made in literacy. For example, book logs (comments about books) that are kept by students over the year can reflect the degree to which students are building positive attitudes and habits regarding reading. Developing positive attitudes and habits, and increasing the ability to construct meaning, are often seen as major goals for a reading program.

Portfolios can consist of a wide variety of materials, including teacher notes, teacher-completed checklists, student self-reflections, reading logs, sample journal pages, written summaries, audiotapes of retellings or oral readings, and videotapes of group projects.

An important element of portfolio assessment—and one that distances it from traditional grading—is that it actively involves students in the process of assessment.

Portfolios are effective in providing teachers with a lot of information on which to base instructional decisions, and from which to evaluate student progress. They are also a good way to communicate students' progress to parents.

Chapter 6

Homework

Homework is the schoolwork students are expected to do at home. There are many valid reasons for teachers to assign homework to students. Those who defend giving students work to do at home believe it can have the following benefits:

- review and practice concepts and skills learned in class;

- prepare for complex or difficult lessons;

- develop better study habits and skills for higher education;

- provide additional time for the exploration of a topic;

- enhance and supplement learning;

- develop time management skills; and,

- foster independent learning.

Aida Fastag-Carvajal, a retired bilingual coordinator, explains that homework is supposed to be a review of what the child has learned. She says that parents should not need to help their children with homework, but they need to make sure that the children do it. "If a parent has to constantly help their child with homework or if he/she always has to explain it to the child, it indicates that there are some serious problems. That's a sign that the parent has to go to school and talk to the teacher. It is possible that the teacher didn't do a good enough job teaching. This should not be the first conclusion that one comes to. There may be other reasons why a child does not understand the assignments. It is best to establish good, open communication with the teacher to explore the reasons for the problem." In the event that the teacher is not receptive to your concerns, you have to approach the principal.

The amount of homework students are assigned every day varies enormously across grade levels, schools, school districts, and states. Some students come home with hours of work to be done for the following day, while others are assigned little to no work to be done at home. It really depends on the school and the teacher.

For example, in recent years, the Piscataway School Board in New Jersey voted to accept ninety minutes of homework as reasonable for middle school students each evening, and up to two hours for high school students.

Other school districts throughout the country followed Piscataway by establishing policies to limit homework assignments. Although the guidelines vary, most are similar to the endorsement made by the National PTA (Parent Teacher Association **www.pta.org**) and NEA (National Education Association **www.nea.org**), which specified an amount of ten minutes per grade level per day. (In fifth grade, for example, it would be 50 minutes a day.)

In recent years, homework has increased due to several situations. Higher academic standards in most states have forced teachers to teach more content during the school year, which cannot always be covered during school hours. Also, the trend to compare U.S. students with those from other countries has contributed to the consensus that U.S. students don't study as much as others, and will continue to fall behind if something is not done about it.

> Marjorie Venegas, an ESL teacher, explains that teachers expect parents to be more involved with their children's homework up to 3rd or 4th grade. After that, kids should be responsible for their own work. Parents are expected to do reading assignments with their kids, and be involved in any art project and, to some extent, in science projects.

When it comes to your children's homework, you should find out how much homework your children have, how long it will take, when it is due, how its grade is going to reflect on the overall grade, and finally, supervise that the homework is done. You are not supposed to be doing your children's homework, but you are supposed to make sure that it is being done and helping when appropriate. Always praise your children when they do a good job!

Homework Help

If you do not speak English or if you cannot help your children with some of the assignments, ask about any after-school program in your children's school or at a local community center that helps children with homework. Many of these community programs are based on income, so they may be free or charge a small fee.

Many states offer help on the phone and online through a program called Dial-A-Teacher. You can ask or submit your homework question in writing and get an answer from volunteer teachers who are available usually from 3:30 to 7:00 p.m. Visit **www.dial-a-teacher.com**, or check with your school for a local telephone number or website.

Keep in mind that the fact that you may not be able to personally help your children does not except you from:

- trying to get someone else to help;

- being aware of your children's project deadlines or homework assignments; and,

- supervising that they finish their homework every day.

Remember that school may be a difficult experience for your children if they have not been in this country for long. Being able to turn in homework on time will not only contribute to their success, but to their sense of worth and self-esteem. Understanding your children's homework may be hard for you—as it is for most parents—but, if you feel you cannot help them, find someone who can. It could be an after-school program, Dial-A-Teacher, a neighbor, another kid who does well in school, a relative, or even help online.

The following are a few websites you may want to check out.

- **www.refdesk.com** offers links to websites for various subjects in all grade levels from 1–12

- **www.math.com** offers math help

- **www.infoplease.com** offers information in all subjects; ideal for middle school and up

- **www.national geographic.com/ homework** offers homework help in the areas of nature, science, animals, plants, maps, history, culture, and art

Appropriate Homework Environment

In the evening, a home can be a very busy place. There are usually adults preparing a meal, someone watching television, another person fixing something that is broken, or someone straightening up the different rooms.

Felix Flores, Assistant Principal at Brookside School in Ossining, New York, comments that the school expects parents to provide a good environment where students can do their homework. This means:

- *a quiet, clean, and well-lit area (which means no television, no siblings yelling, and no adults talking at the kitchen table if that is where the homework is being done);*

- *a comfortable chair, and table or desk;*

- *a specifically assigned time to do homework when they are not expected to do anything else but homework; and,*

- *a computer. If you cannot afford one, make sure you bring your child to the local public library where they usually have several available.*

Mr. Flores adds that parents need to be available to answer questions, but you should avoid giving your children the answer to a problem that they need to resolve on their own. The best way for you to help your children work through a problem is by breaking it into smaller steps.

There are people walking in and out, errands to run, and phone calls to make. This hectic activity can make it very hard for children to concentrate in order to study or to do homework that needs to be completed for the following day. This is why it is important to establish a clear time and place for homework that tells the children how seriously the family takes their school work.

NOTE: Regarding computers, keep in mind that there is currently a wide educational gap between children who have access to technology and children who do not. A computer is a basic tool for school work and for future job readiness. You can get them at excellent prices and with all sorts of financing. Consider it a needed investment in your children's future.

Cultural Tip

Maybe you work long hours or at several jobs to support your family. Perhaps sometimes you do not have anyone to watch your children when they come home from school, so you take them with you to your evening job. Keep in mind that these kids suffer from poor sleep and usually lag behind in their schoolwork. If this is your situation, consider the following:

• make arrangements for your children to sleep over at a relative's home on the nights you work;

• call the Social Services Department and find out if you qualify for available child care services; or,

• establish a homework area at your job so your children can sit and work.

Chapter 7
Parental Involvement

All the research and the experts agree that when parents are involved, children perform better in school. There are several reasons for this, the first one being the fact that you send a positive message to your children that you care about their education, that school is important to you, and therefore, it becomes important to them. It is also true that schools pay more attention to children whose parents are involved because they make their expectations known, so teachers and others can work towards those expectations. Another important point is that if you are involved, you know what your children should be learning and can follow their progress on a daily basis, which enables you to catch problems early.

Claire Sylvan, Executive Director of the Internationals Network for Public Schools, formerly International Partnership Schools, in New York, New York, reminds you that middle school children are experiencing a lot of changes. They need to find a supportive environment that enables them to bond with other children, and they also need a strong family that can help them resist bad influences. It is important for you to connect with other people in the community who share high expectations for your children.

Parent involvement is not just for the early grades. Staying involved with your children's education through middle school and high school is crucial for their success.

Cultural Tip

Latinos often tend to shy away from their children's school, either out of fear or out of a belief that education is best left up to teachers. It does not work like that here. The more involved you are, the better it is for your children. Socialize with other parents and become part of the school community. It will do wonders for your children's self-esteem and educational progress.

There are many ways of getting involved, the main one being that you know your children's teachers and how to reach them. You should also know the principal, the guidance counselor, and the ESL teacher. You must attend parent/teacher conferences and any special meetings the school calls for. It will also be wonderful for your children if you could volunteer at the school.

Marjorie Venegas, an ESL Teacher, comments that school is a great place for parents to learn about the American culture. "You can meet other parents, find out what they do, what they think, and also learn about your rights."

When you get involved and you learn your rights, you become a better advocate for your children. You can get things done. For example, even if you are told that there is no room for your children in the school, you can find them seats; you can place them in a bilingual program that you prefer; and, you can demand to have an interpreter in a parent/teacher conference. You will find a complete list of your rights and responsibilities in Chapter 12.

Cultural Tip

Some schools or individuals within the school may have lower expectations of minority students. When this occurs, your children will not be challenged as much as other students. This in turn will reflect on their achievement level, as well as on their self-esteem. If you are involved in your children's education, you will notice these issues, and you can immediately address them with the appropriate person.

Volunteering

In the United States, there is a culture of volunteering that many Latinos never experienced before. People volunteer at all sorts of organizations, and parents who are concerned about their children's education often volunteer in their children's schools where there are plenty of opportunities to volunteer. You can be part of the PTA or PTO of the school (Parent Teacher Association or Organization, a nonprofit group that exists in every school and that groups parents and teachers together). You can help with their fund-raising activities, their programs, or their governance. You can also volunteer to help the teacher in the classroom, to accompany your children's classes on field trips, to do recess duty, or help in the office. Just let the principal know that you wish to volunteer, and tell him or her how much time you have available. In the last few years, some very good schools have implemented a policy that in order for parents to enroll their child, they need to sign up for a certain number of volunteer hours.

As we said earlier, there are many reasons why some parents are not involved with their children's education. It may be because they do not understand the education system or because they feel it is better to leave education to schools. Others may have no time because they work hard. Whatever your situation, you should always stay in touch with the school through notes, phone calls to the teacher, and with your children at home. Also, keep in mind that regardless of your level of involvement, one thing you need to try hard to do is attend all parent/teacher conferences. Read more about them in the next chapter.

In 2004, Cornestone at Pedregal Elementary School in Rancho Palos Verdes, California, won the prestigious Blue Ribbon Award for Community Involvement. Its principal, Jodi Pastell, is convinced that its model can be replicated in all other schools. "I ask parents who want to enroll their children in my school to commit to 3.5 hours of volunteer work per week. The strong partnership between teachers and parents is the key to children's progress, which is tracked with standard-based report cards every trimester." Working along with the teachers, parents help create a warm, nurturing, and safe environment for students to excel.

Ms. Pastell says that one of the most serious problems she noticed in Latino parents when she taught bilingual school in New Mexico was their lack of involvement with the education system.

Checking the Backpack

Make a habit of checking your children's book bags every day when they return from school. This is important to avoid missing any notes the school might have sent you. You cannot use the excuse "I did not know" if the school sends you notes that you do not read. Talk to the principal or the teacher if you need the notes to be in Spanish.

Checking the book bags also has another purpose. It will alert you right away of anything strange in it, whether there are things that do not belong to your children (and that they may have stolen), or things they should not be around (such as cigarettes, matches, drugs, or weapons).

John Diamond, a sociologist and assistant professor at Harvard Graduate School of Education, points out that some educators assume that Latino parents do not have the time, the resources, or the talent to be involved with their children's school. Therefore, they do not reach out to parents because they think they have very little to offer. In order to break with this stereotype, you need to show up at the school often, talk to the principal and the teachers, volunteer, express your expectations for your children, and let them know that you want to be informed of your children's progress. If you cannot be at the school as often as you would like, you should let teachers and administrators know that you are committed to your children's education and that you want to be informed about what they are doing in school. "Communication is key to breaking the stereotypes," explains Dr. Diamond.

Chapter 8

Parent/Teacher Conference

At least twice a year, the school will hold a parent/teacher conference. They are usually twenty minutes long, and it is very important for you to attend. It is an opportunity for you to meet with your children's teachers, find out about your children's progress and any difficulties, and express your concerns and your satisfaction with your children's work.

Generally, the students are not present at the conference. It is a time for the parents and teachers to meet to discuss how everything is going. In some schools the children will be present, but given other activities while the parents and teachers talk. In some middle schools and high schools, students are now being invited to participate at the parent/teacher conference. Being present gives them a stronger sense of responsibility for their learning.

Remember that if you do not speak English, you have the right to ask for an interpreter. If your children are present, do not use them to translate, because they may "edit" what either you or the teacher is saying. You should also ask that the interpreter translates everything that is being said and avoid editorializing for you.

What To Do Before the Conference

To take full advantage of this meeting with your children's teachers, prepare for it as if you were attending an important meeting at work. There are a few things you could do to help prepare.

- Ask your children if they have any concerns or questions they would like for you to discuss with their teachers.

- Talk with your children about their schedules.

- Find out about your children's most and least favorite subjects and activities.

What To Bring To the Conference

Before the conference, it would be wise to prepare some notes of the topics you wish to discuss, as well as some information you need to share with the teacher. For example:

- your children's report card from the previous year if they changed schools;

- a list of subjects each of your children enjoy;

- a list of allergies any of your children might have;

- any recent changes in your children's life, such as the death of a close relative, parents' divorce, or illness; or,

- extracurricular activities your children are involved in.

Keep in mind that you want to establish a good rapport with the teachers, so opening the meeting with an expression of your gratitude for their job is a good idea. If you have positive details regarding your children's work in school that you are particularly happy about, this is a good time to share them.

> Claire Sylvan shares her own personal strategy as a mother: "Every time I visit a teacher I first tell her how much my son loves her class. Only after that I bring up my questions or concerns." As was said before, it is important to open the meeting focusing on a positive fact about the teacher and his or her class.

Important Questions to Ask

The parent/teacher conference is a unique opportunity for you to ask key questions that will help you understand your children's school performance, any areas of concerns, and ideas you could implement at home to contribute to their success. The following is a list of some questions you may want to ask.

- How is my child doing?

- In what area is he or she doing well? Can you show me evidence?

- Where does he or she need improvement? Can you show me?

- Does my child participate in class? Does he or she answer questions? Is he or she shy?

- How does he or she behave?

- Do you suspect any hearing or speech problems? (If that's the case: Who can I talk about available services?)

- What is he or she supposed to be learning in this grade?

- Is my child doing all the homework on a regular basis?

- How much do you expect me to help with his or her homework? (If you do not speak English, ask how your child can get help if he or she needs it.)

- How do you assess my child? Through tests? Portfolios? Class participation?

- Which tests will be administered during the school year and for what purposes? What are my child's test dates?

- How will the results of the test be used?

- What does an "F" mean? (A lot of kids tell their Spanish-speaking parents that an "F" means "fine.")

- Should my child practice taking tests?

- Do you know what my child's special talents are? Would you be able to tell me how to help him or her develop those talents further?

- What can I do specifically to help?

- Is my child attending school every day?

- With how many absences will the child fail class or be suspended?

- How can I get in touch with you? (Also, give the teacher your updated numbers.)

After the Conference

It is a good idea to thank the teacher for his or her time. You can write a note or call. Continue to be in touch with the teachers through the year, even if your children are doing well. When your children know that you and their teachers are in touch all the time, they will see education as a priority.

Talk to your children about the points that were brought up at the conference. Stress the good ones first and mention anything that needs improvement. Also, share with your children any action plan you may have discussed with the teachers to help achieve their goals.

Chapter 9

Preparing Your Children to Enter School

Earlier, when parent involvement was discussed, the main topic was involvement with your children's education once they are already in school. The truth is that your involvement with your children's education should start much earlier than that.

There are many concepts that have to be taught at home when children are 2, 3, and 4 years old in order to contribute to their maturity by the time they enter school. Making sure your children acquire certain skills early on will give them a better chance to succeed in school.

Preparing Children to Read and Write

You should be aware that children develop the concept of time and space when they are between 3 and 5 years old. Helping your kids internalize this abstract concept through specific everyday activities will greatly help them when they arrive in kindergarten and they first approach reading and writing.

Dr. Iris Yankelevich, a psychotherapist who specializes in family therapy, suggests activities such as the following: "When you are putting away the laundry, point out: 'You see, the socks go in this drawer and the panties go in this other one.' This way, you will help your child understand that there is a place for everything. This skill is the same skill the child will need when learning to read. By then, children will have an easy time understanding that the letter 'm' goes in front of the letter 'o' in order to read 'mom.' This will also help them understand that sounds follow each other and they will be able to place the different sounds in a word."

Dr. Yankelevich stresses that when parents do not read to their children—no matter in what language—children arrive in school without these important skills and fall behind other children. "The lack of these abilities is the reason why many Latino children never make the leap from reading mechanically to understanding what they read," Dr. Yankelevich explains.

There are other prerequisites to learning how to read. Many Latino parents who do not read English refuse to read Spanish books to their children, thinking that they will confuse them and that their kids will have trouble learning English. The opposite is actually true. When you read a story in Spanish to your children and you ask them to retell it to you, you are aiding them in developing many skills, such as memory, concentration, attention, expression, association, deduction, and induction. These last three are reasoning processes. Children can easily transfer all these skills to English once they learn the language in school.

Communicate with Your Children

There is one more thing you should keep in mind—try to avoid giving orders as the only means of communication with your children. Children whose parents do not talk to them arrive in school with poor language skills. No matter what language you speak, talk to your children. Converse with them, tell them stories, ask them to tell you stories, play oral games, and sing songs with them. It will help them be more prepared for school.

Preparing Your Children for Math

Introducing your kids to math concepts before they reach school age is equally important. It is crucial that you expose them to these ideas when they are 2, 3 and 4 years old.

Again, the best thing you can do is to approach the concepts in a very practical way. For example, as you take your children to the supermarket, ask them to grab two apples and then two pears. Then ask them how many pieces of fruit you have now. When children see the practical application of math concepts, they internalize them in a natural way. By the time they get to school, not only do they understand these ideas easily, but they are more interested in math because they have seen the practical use of it.

Preparing Your Children for Social Interaction

In the last few years children have been spending an increased amount of time playing with video games, the computer, their iPods, and watching television. All of these activities have isolated them from other kids, and when they arrive in school (and then throughout their school years into adulthood) they lack basic social skills, such as tolerance, the ability to dialogue and negotiate, and acceptance of others. You can read more about the effects of this trend in Chapter 11.

To counteract these tendencies, limit the amount of time your children spend involved with video games, television, and the computer, and increase the amount of time they spend in non-directed activities. This means that, although it is important for children to be involved in sports and different kinds of classes, it is also important for them to just play with no adult around telling them what to do. This gives them a chance to figure out solutions to problems that may arise on their own. Take them to the park to meet other kids, and let them get together with friends at your house or their friend's house.

Cultural Tip

A lot of Latino parents think that their children are wasting their time when they are just playing with other kids. This is the reason why they don't consider play dates or sleepovers important. However, they are a basic way for children to develop their social skills and learn how to interact with others. Americans value these activities greatly, and it would help your kids with their assimilation process if you learned to value them as well.

Good Habits Start at Home

Food is such a powerful cultural thing that many parents continue to eat and feed their families the same food they ate in their native countries. However, even though you might think you are feeding them the same food you grew up with, it is very doubtfully actually the same. The entire food process (from planting to packaging) in this country is most likely different from what you were used to. During this process, otherwise healthy and nutritious food loses a lot of its nutrients. In exchange, food manufacturers add chemicals, hormones, antibiotics, and other items you may not be aware of.

That is why it is important for you to add a variety of items to your family's diet to make sure you are providing them with all the nutrients needed to grow.

The other side effect of teaching your children to eat healthy and making them conscious of what is good for them and what is not, is that as they grow and reach the difficult pre-teenage and teenage years, they will be better equipped to resist drugs and alcohol. As children become aware of the products that enter their body, they build psychological resistance to substances that will harm them.

Dr. Yankelevich mentions research done a few years ago that highlighted a higher difficulty in understanding math in children who lacked iron. "Iron is found in green leafed vegetables, in split peas, and in everything red: tomatoes, apples, and beets. It is also recommended that parents double the dose of iron for girls once they begin menstruating, because they lose iron during those days and it has been proven that that may be the reason why they can have more trouble in math than boys at that age."

Cultural Tip

Maybe when you were growing up, sodas were a luxury in your country, something that you drank only occasionally. Now that you have easy access to them, you are happy to let your kids drink them all the time. Keep in mind that sodas and a lot of juices are full of sugar and chemicals that are not good for your children's health. The best thing you can do for your children to develop healthy habits is to help them get used to drinking water.

For more information on issues related to parenting your Latino children, check Dr. Iris Yankelevich's book, *Padres de hoy (How to be parents today)* from Llewellyn Publishing.

Chapter 10

Activities to Help Your Child Succeed in School

The previous chapter focused on helping your children get ready to enter school. This chapter is dedicated to all those activities you can do to help them be successful once they are in school.

In today's competitive world, everything you can do to help your children do well in school will benefit them in the long run. Remember that having a well-rounded education will definitely give your children more options for the future.

There are many fun things you can either do with your children or encourage them to do on their own. In the following pages, you will find many suggestions broken down according to the different skills they will help develop.

Maria Guasp, principal research analyst at the American Institute for Research, and a former principal and superintendent of New York City and California schools, reminds us that as a parent, you are your children's first teacher; therefore, everything you do with your children can be helpful.

Keep in mind that you will need to adapt the suggestions offered below to your children's ages. Do not be shy about trying new things with your children, because they enjoy a wide variety of activities. Remember, children are like sponges—they absorb everything around them.

Encourage Language Development

An important part of maturing is to develop the ability to express thoughts, ideas, and feelings. It is an ability children will need to succeed in school and in life. When children spend too much time by themselves in front of a computer, video game, or television, they are less exposed to social interactions that enable them to develop communication skills. They have trouble expressing themselves clearly and understanding what others mean. They may also have difficulties understanding what they read.

In order to encourage the development of this very crucial skill, you may want to try some of the following activities recommended by Dr. Guasp.

- Ask questions and allow your children to give you a complete answer. Do not finish their sentences for them.

- Listen and pay close attention to your children when they talk. Look at them and focus on what they say.

- Limit the time your children watch television, as well as what they watch. Make what they watch personal—ask why they like it (or do not like it), and ask them to anticipate the ending.

■ Limit the time your children spend on their cell phones and playing video games.

■ Sing and make music together.

■ Play board games and puzzles together.

■ Make time for storytelling. Tell stories of your childhood and about your family. Have them tell you made-up stories.

■ Have your children write in a journal.

■ Point at signs on the street and ask if they know the word or the first letter of the word.

■ Ask what their day was like in school.

■ Read to your children every day in Spanish or in English. After you finish reading, ask questions like the following.

　■ Do you sometimes feel like the character in the story?

　■ How would you change the ending?

　■ Can you imagine how the story would change if it were told from a different point of view? (For example, if "Little Red Riding Hood" had been written from the Wolf's perspective?)

■ Have your children read to you or to a younger sibling every day.

- Have many children's books at home in Spanish and in English.

- Get a library card so you can borrow books, videos, and CDs from the public library.

- Read hymns at church.

- Model reading behavior. Read the newspaper, magazines, recipes, cereal boxes, and so on. When your children see you reading, they will want to imitate you.

- Share interesting articles you read with your children.

- Write notes for your children and put them in their bags or lunch boxes.

You can find many more reading activities in the bilingual book *¡Leamos!/Let's read*, by Mary and Richard Behm, published by New Concepts in Learning.

Cultural Tip

Reading to your children in your native language will give them a sense of belonging, and will help them value their family language and culture. Children who are read to, even if it is in Spanish, do much better in school, because they can easily transfer the language skills to English.

Help your Children Develop Math Skills

As discussed in an earlier section, math entails the understanding of abstract concepts, and some children have difficulty grasping it. If you show them the practical use of math, they will be more interested in learning it in school.

- Get your children to help you when you are counting money or giving back change at a store.

- Get your children to help you with decisions you make when you shop, like figuring out if this is cheaper than that and which item is a better value.

- Ask your children to read the directions of a recipe you are making and get them to help you measure ingredients.

- Help your children average the score of their favorite players.

- Play dominoes, Monopoly, and other board games that are math-related.

- Make sure your children know math vocabulary. They should try to explain to you any new concepts, so you can verify that they understood.

Help your Children Develop Science Skills

So many areas in life are infused with science. When you share exciting activities at home that are science related, your children will make the connection between theory and practice, and they will be more enthusiastic about learning the theory.

- Build models with your children.

- Teach them how to repair things around the house, from a ceramic bowl to a toaster oven.

- Borrow a book from the library on constellations, and then watch the stars at night and try to identify them.

- Borrow books from the library on fish and then take a trip to the fish store to identify different species (or just go fishing and try to identify the fish you catch).

- Take a walk in the park and write down as many animals as you encounter. Then go home and look for information on their habitats, eating habits, and so on.

- Depending on your children's ages, cut out articles from the newspaper regarding scientific matters, such as DNA testing that enables police to find criminals, Virgin Intergalactic's plans for future space trips with regular passengers, and so on.

Help your Children Develop Social Skills and Widen their View of the World

A recent study has shown that children who finish high school lack some fundamental social skills needed to enter the workforce. Dr. Iris Yankelevich believes that this lack of social skills is connected with the fact that children have been holding a remote control in their hands for most of their growing years. Now they see relationships as a game about how much control they can have. Needless to say, this is not the right attitude to succeed in the world.

As a parent, you can help them acquire these abilities by engaging them in conversations and in social interactions of all kinds, with family, friends, and acquaintances.

- Talk about different careers and different jobs.

- Take trips. All trips are important, whether you go to another borough, uptown, or out of town. They create situations and expose children to different experiences, such as riding on the subway or on a bus, visiting a park or the zoo, and going to the beach or to a busy city. Show your children a map of the place you are going to visit and point out how you will get there. Use these opportunities to spark conversations. Ask your children to write about the trip after you return.

- Organize play dates for your children so they learn to socialize with children their age outside of school.

- Organize a sleepover and send your children to their friends' houses to sleep over.

- Enroll your children in any of the after-school programs offered by Boys and Girls Clubs or the YMCA. They offer a wide variety of classes, from ballet classes to drama and swimming. Usually they charge on a sliding scale, so they may be more affordable than you think. To find a club near your home, visit **www.bgca.org**.

- Enroll your children in a summer camp. Besides a large selection of private programs that range from tennis or soccer camps to musical ones, there are many agencies that offer free summer camps. Find out about them through your school social worker or psychologist.

- Take your children on camping trips with friends, or let them go on camping trips (and other trips) with other families and their children.

Help your Children Develop Healthy Lifestyle Habits

The importance of good nutrition and good eating habits was talked about in Chapter 9. To reinforce the benefits that are associated with your children being more conscious about which foods are good and which ones are bad for them:

1) they will be healthier;

2) healthier children do better in school; and,

3) children who are aware of what they put inside their bodies are better prepared to resist drugs and alcohol as they grow up.

So, it is fundamental for you to instill the concepts of healthy lifestyle and good nutrition in your children from a very young age. There are a few things you can do in this regard.

- Talk about healthy foods. Explain the difference between good and bad foods. Set goals for how much sugar your children are allowed each day. Make sure you fill your refrigerator with healthy foods and snacks.

- Look for healthy recipes and cook them together. Children love to cook. Borrow cookbooks from the library or buy a cookbook with exciting recipes.

- Take walks or hikes together.

- Stay physically active yourself so you are a good role model for your children. Encourage your children to engage in physical activity. They should join a sports team or regularly play sports with friends.

Help your Children Develop a Love of Art

Art makes the world a better place. Learning to appreciate art will help your children become more sensitive. It will open their eyes to different points of view, to creativity, and to diversity, all of which can only work toward making them more creative, tolerant, and flexible people.

■ Have colored pencils, crayons, and paper at home, and encourage your children to draw and paint.

■ Check your local paper for free events, such as performances by local theater companies, art exhibits, film screenings, fairs, farmers market, or concerts.

■ Visit museums and exhibitions together. Ask your children what they see and what they feel. Visit the museum's gift shop and buy inexpensive posters to put in the children's rooms.

■ Frame and hang all artwork produced by your children.

Cultural Tip

You may think that you should discourage your children from going into a career in art, given that in many Latin American countries, an art career means starving. In the United States, however, there are many profitable careers that are art-related, such as fashion design, packaging design, art dealing, and graphic design. Instead of going against your children's vocation, try to work with them towards an art career that offers good job opportunities.

Chapter 11

High School

If your children were raised in a Latin American country, the prospect of entering high school in America could be a scary one. High schools in this country are usually large and crowded, and the way they work is quite different from their counterparts in South America. So, I suggest that you provide your children all the support they need through this period.

The process of choosing a high school is similar to the one for choosing an elementary school. You need to ask a lot of questions in order to find the school that best suits your children's needs and future plans. Talk to your local librarian, other parents, teachers, and people from the community.

When you do your research, consider the following issues.

- Is the size of the school appropriate for your children? Is it too big or overcrowded? Would they feel better in a smaller school?

- Does the school have a specialty (technology, arts, math)?

- What is the ethnic make up of the school?

- What percentage of the students graduate every year?

- What percentage of students who graduated go to college?

- How does this school rate in violent incidents compared to other schools in the area?

- Is the school environment friendly and challenging to students?

- Is there a sense of community?

- Do teachers have a history of supporting students?

Parent Involvement in High School

High school is a very difficult time for children, and even more so if they were not raised in this country. They are more independent, they are searching for their identity, their need to belong to a group is exacerbated, and they are willing to try different things. They are also more susceptible to bad influences. All good reasons for you to remain involved in their education.

At this level, one of the areas you should be involved with is the balance between their social life and their school work. As important as it is to encourage your children spending time with other youngsters, high school is also a time to focus on hard work. Grades are increasingly important for your children to have more opportunities to go to the colleges they choose.

Learn About Key Exams and Programs

There are many important exams and programs that will improve a student's potential for succeeding in college.

PSAT Test

Educators highly recommend that your 10th grader take the PSAT exams. PSAT stands for Preliminary Scholastic Assessment Test. It is a standardized test that provides firsthand practice for the Scholastic Assessment Test (SAT) Reasoning Test.

The PSAT measures:

- critical reading skills;

- math problem-solving skills; and,

- writing skills.

Keep in mind that students have developed these skills over many years, both in and out of school. There are many reasons for encouraging your children to take this test, but the following are the most important ones.

- To receive feedback on your children's strengths and weaknesses on skills necessary for college study.

- To see how your children's performance on an admissions test might compare with that of others applying to college.

- To enter the competition for scholarships from the National Merit Scholarship Corporation (which is awarded in grade 11).

- To help prepare for the SAT, the results of which are used as part of the college application process. Your children can become familiar with the kinds of questions and the exact directions they will see on the SAT.

Advanced Placement Programs

Along with the results of the PSAT, the teacher gets what is called an Advanced Placement (AP) potential for each student, telling him or her which students are the most likely to do well in college. If your children are amongst them, they can enroll in an AP program where they will be able to take courses that will prepare them for the type of work done in college. They can also earn credits towards college.

Not all schools offer AP classes, so talk to your principal. In the event that they are not offered in your children's school, find out if they can participate online. Go to the College Board (the publisher of the test) website at **www.collegeboard.com** for more information.

As a parent, it is important for you to help your children in the process of deciding whether they should take advance placement courses. It involves hard work, but it has many benefits for your children, and you can help them see these benefits:

- get a head start on college-level work;

- improve their writing skills and sharpen their problem-solving techniques;

- develop the study habits necessary for tackling rigorous course work;

- stand out in the college admissions process;

- demonstrate maturity and readiness for college;

- show willingness to push themselves to the limit;

- explore the world from a variety of perspectives, including their own;

- study subjects in greater depth and detail; and,

- assume the responsibility of reasoning, analyzing, and understanding for themselves.

It is a well-known fact that students who take AP courses do better in college and in their career. If it is offered, your children should pursue this opportunity.

SATs and ACTs

Regarding the SAT, the only difference from the PSAT is the format. The type of questions and techniques that apply to the PSAT also apply to the SAT.

The SAT is administered seven times a year—usually in October, November, December, January, March, May, and June—on Saturday mornings. The ACT, a test similar to the SAT, is administered six times a year—usually September, October, December, February, April, and June—also on Saturday mornings. To find out more details about the SAT, visit the College Board website at **www.collegeboard.com**. For more information on the ACT, visit the ACT Inc. website (the publisher of the ACT) at **www.act.org**. Both sites have a Spanish section where you can read details about the test.

It is crucial that your children take either the SAT or the ACT, because even though colleges may consider other factors, the majority of admission decisions are based on only two criteria—the child's SAT or ACT score and GPA (grade point average).

The experts say that many Latino parents are not aware of the importance of sending their children to SAT and ACT preparation courses where they learn how to take the test. You have to keep in mind that these tests requires certain skills that children may not have, even if they are great students.

Despite the fact that students can take either one of these tests as often as they want (even though some schools will average their scores), most people are better off preparing thoroughly for the test, taking it once, and getting their top score. You or your children should call the universities to which they will be applying to find out their policy on multiple scores.

Cultural Tip

You may feel that your children are already doing much better than you did in your country, and that they are better off finding a job or joining the family business instead of attending college. Be aware that more and more jobs in this country require a higher level of skills than those provided by a high school education. If your children do not seek a college degree, their chances of succeeding financially in the United States will be drastically reduced.

Tracking

Tracking means that students are grouped according to their ability in a particular subject. For example, there may be two different math classes—a low track and a high track. Although some tracking takes places in many elementary and middle schools as well, high school is usually when students are tracked.

In recent years, there has been a lot of controversy over the tracking of students' abilities, because some research shows that minorities are disproportionately represented in the lower track. Because these lower tracks have been shown to lead to lower achievement in later years, it is important that you become informed about this issue.

Some experts believe that grouping students according to their abilities helps the high-track students, because they get better teachers who can challenge them with more difficult material, whereas it is less beneficial to low-track students who are not pushed hard enough. Other experts think that on the contrary, when students of homogeneous abilities are in the same class (which is what tracking does), they learn more because the material is targeted to their level.

One thing is true—the children of parents who are on top of this issue (who get help in math and science for their children, and who talk to the teacher about how their children can improve in these curricular areas) tend to be placed in higher tracks. Because educated parents are very aware of how much the high tracks have helped them in their educational careers, they are the most vocal about having their children placed in the high track. That is why, in order to give your child more opportunities, you need to become well-versed on this topic. If your children's school tracks students, ask your PTA for literature on the subject.

Some Worrisome Statistics

You need to know that the high school completion rate for Latinos is much lower than that of all other populations. According to 2001 data from the National Center for Education Statistics of the United States Education Department, the percentage of 18- to 24-year-old Caucasians who have a high school diploma is around 90%; for Asian/Pacific Islanders is around 96%; for African-Americans is around 85%; and, for Latinos is 65%.

According to the White House Initiative on Education Excellence for Hispanic Americans, one in every three

Hispanic students does not complete high school, and only 10% of Hispanics graduate from four-year colleges and universities.

According to the Pew Hispanic Center, by the time they are 26 years old, 43% of Hispanic dropouts have received a GED (a high school equivalency diploma), compared to 50% of white dropouts.

Although there are several theories regarding this educational gap, there are a number of reasons that can contribute to these appalling statistics.

- Students see limited job possibilities after high school because jobs are not available where they live. They may think education does not pay off.

- Minority students may feel alienated from the school context. They do not feel validated, because their cultural background is not understood or embraced by the school. Their second language is not seen as strength.

- Students may see opportunities to get into the workforce now, and they may not see that the

Abe Tomás Hughes II, CEO of Hispanic Alliance for Career Enhancement (HACE), was born to Mexican parents in a border town. He is the only one of four siblings who went to college and graduated with an MBA from Harvard. "In Latin America there is a caste system. If you were born poor, it's very difficult to get out of poverty because there is very little social mobility. That's the difference with the U.S., where if you study, you can change your socioeconomic status. I see it in my own family; I look back on my life and I see how different it is from that of my siblings. They live week to week, they've gone through several divorces, had children out of wedlock, and their teenage granddaughters are becoming pregnant."

long-term consequence of not having a high school diploma is a lack of upper-mobility.

- Children do not feel successful in school. They do not have ties with adults—teachers or guidance counselors—who could make them feel successful. They would rather get out and find something to do where they can feel good about themselves.

- They do not feel a sense of community at school. They feel a sense of community with a gang or at home.

- Parents believe that education is important, but that making money is more important.

How to Help Your Child Stay in School and Out of Trouble

In the last few years, statistics have shown that more and more Latino kids drop out of school—or they never enter school if they are recent immigrants—to join a gang. The fast growth of urban gangs is worrying authorities and parents alike.

Confronted with a lack of sense of community and belonging, young people look for an alternative that can end up being a very bad choice.

How do you make sure your children do not get involved with the wrong people? For starters, you must talk to them and learn to listen to your children. Talk to them when they are young, and never stop communicating. Always try to find out about their interests, their concerns, their dreams and their fears. Make them feel loved, important, and worthy. Be aware that one of the reasons children join gangs is to "be someone," to do something noteworthy. Do not give them the chance to need to be someone in a dangerous environment. Help them reach their best potential by staying in school.

Obviously, the best way to help your high school children stay in school is by staying involved with their education. Do not think that because they want their independence, you should back off completely and ignore what is happening in school.

Teenagers deal with a lot of psychological and physical changes, peer pressure, and emotional ups and downs. It is important as a parent that you show them your strength and support, and most of all, that you love them and are interested in their well-being.

There are a many things you can do to increase the chances of your children staying in school and doing well in their studies, while at the same time, staying out of trouble.

- Look for smaller schools where instruction is more personalized. This will help your children feel supported and challenged.

- Look for schools where a second language and Latino culture are valued and considered pluses, not minuses, and where they will not be teased or worse, discriminated.

- Beware of your children's strengths and weaknesses in each subject early on, so you can get your children the help they need.

- Beware of test dates and preparation requirements.

- Make your house the place where your children hang out with friends. This way, you will meet your children's friends and you will be able to better control where your children are and how they spend their time.

- Participate in school fairs, fund raisers, and so on, just as you would with your younger children.

- Make it a habit of going to school and finding out your children's attendance, behavior, and grades, even when the school doesn't call you. The teacher may tell you that your children are too quiet, or that they do not have friends. This may indicate to you that there is something happening that you may not have noticed at home.

- Establish strict rules and limits. Although they rebel against them, teenagers need and want limits. It shows them that you care about them. For example, as mentioned earlier, limit the amount of time they spend watching television, surfing the Internet, or chatting on the phone. Many teenagers stay up until very late at night and do not get enough sleep. This will in turn affect their grades, and eventually, their school attendance.

- Try to keep a balance between being your children's friend and being their parent. Parents who are just friends of their kids have a hard time parenting them.

The best way to help your children stay in school, how-ever, is to catch any signs of trouble early on. Doing that requires close attention on your part and a willing-ness to modify some of your own behavior whenever necessary.

For starters, you should always observe any changes in your children's behavior, how they dress, their eating habits, and their sleep pat-terns. The key of your obser-vation is that you should avoid any criticism. When you criticize children, you push them away. They will imple-ment their changes without you knowing about them. For instance, they will leave the expensive clothes they bought with drug money at a friend's house, and you will not find out about it.

> According to Gustavo Iaies, a well-known sociologist, the democratization of family rela-tionships have made it tougher for parents to exercise their authority at home. Beware that your children need you to exer-cise this authority, and so does the school.

So, if you see any changes, ask your children questions like, "Do you feel more secure wearing a bandana?" or "Do you feel you have to wear those baggy pants because the other kids wear them?" There is a big pos-sibility that some of the changes your children are experimenting with have to do with their age, and not with the fact that they have joined a gang or gotten into trouble.

The same is true if your children's grades begin to drop. Explore the cause instead of criticizing or punishing them. Ask questions, such as, "Do you think you need help in this area?" or "Are you getting enough sleep?"

Many times criticism takes the form of comments, such as "I don't know who you take after! You have nothing in common with me/this family" or "Your grandfather would be so embarrassed by your behavior." Comments like these will make your children feel that they do not belong in the family and are more likely to push them in the wrong direction. Instead, your goal is to show concern and to provide a welcoming environment.

Another area where you might need to modify your own behavior in order to handle teenagers growing up in the United States, is in allowing them to have social time outside of school. Many teenagers feel that they have no time to hang out with their friends outside of school. If you fail to build time in their schedule, they will cut classes and eventually drop out.

> *The experts suggest that you organize fun outings with your family. Find out what your children enjoy and do it as a family. That way, they don't feel that they can only have fun with people outside the family.*

You also need to allow time and privacy for your children to speak on the phone with their friends.

Your Children's Vocations

High school is also a good time for you to begin exploring your children's vocations. By now, you probably know what their talents are. Begin discussing what they would like to study when they finish school. Although their ideas may not agree with what you want them to study, be open. Youngsters who get pressured to follow a certain career (to support the family business for example, or something that is prestigious in your country) tend to rebel by refusing to go to college. Try to understand that a career is something with which your children will have to live for the rest of their lives. It should be their choice.

Having said that, you can guide your children in the process of finding a career that fits their needs and talents. As said before, a career in art, for example, does not necessarily mean they have to starve. You can help them explore interesting artistic careers that will both allow them to express their talents and support themselves. Talk to the career counselor in school for ideas, visit a career center at the local community college, or search on the Internet with your children.

Mr. Hughes, the CEO of HACE, strongly emphasizes the need to go on to college. "There is a big salary difference between people with a high school degree and people with a college degree. And the truth is that anyone can find a four year college because there are all sorts of financing and scholarships to help you." He also believes that if your child is a talented student, you should push him or her to go to one of the top universities for which, by the way, there are also loans and grants available. "That is where they will make all the connections that will open doors for them for the rest of their lives."

Cultural Tip

In the United States, vocation is highly valued. In a competitive market such as this, it is very important for your children to choose a career where they feel the drive to grow and compete. If you force them to follow the career of your dreams, or what is valued in your country, it is very possible that they will not reach their full potential, and in addition, they will be unhappy.

Chapter 12

Parents' Rights and Responsibilities

During the last few years, schools have become increasingly conscious of the importance of parents being an active part of the school community. As we saw on Chapter 7, your involvement does make a difference in the way your children perceive education and its importance in life.

Naturally, when it comes to your children's school and education, there are rights and responsibilities you should be aware of.

Your Rights

Knowing your rights will make you a better advocate for your children. As mentioned earlier, teachers and school administrators are more reactive to parents who know their rights and their children's rights than to those who do not.

- You have a right to know your children's teachers, principal, and all other school personnel.

■ You have a right to know about all special programs your children are enrolled in.

■ You have a right to be notified immediately when your children are not attending school.

■ You have a right to be notified immediately if your children need ESL or bilingual services.

■ You have a right to appeal the placement of your children in a special education class and in an ESL or bilingual class.

■ You have a right to observe your children's classes at any time.

■ You have a right to call the children's teachers and find out how they are doing.

■ You have a right to see your children's records. If the records include test scores, you have a right to see the scores.

■ You have a right to participate in meaningful parent/teacher conferences.

■ You have a right to be informed about important changes in school.

■ You have a right to know about any extended academic support available to your children.

■ You have a right to have an interpreter present during meetings about your children's progress.

- You have a right to be a partner with the school to support your children's education.

Rights of Parents of English as a Second Language Learners

In order to protect children from possible discrimination based on their lack of linguistic ability, if your child is taking English as a Second Language classes, there are a few additional rights that have been granted by the No Child Left Behind Act.

- You have a right to have your children receive a quality education and be taught by a highly qualified teacher.

- You have a right to have your children learn English and other subjects, such as reading, other language arts, and mathematics at the same academic level as all other students.

- You have a right to know if your children have been identified and recommended for placement in an English language acquisition program, and to accept or refuse such placement.

- You have a right to choose a different English language acquisition program for your children, if one is available.

- You have a right to transfer your children to another school if the current school is identified as "in need of improvement."

- You have a right to apply for supplemental services, such as tutoring, for your children if the current school is identified as "in need of improvement" for two years.

- You have a right to have your children tested annually to assess their progress in English language acquisition.

- You have a right to receive information regarding your children's performance on academic tests.

- You have a right to have your children taught with programs that are scientifically proven to work.

- You have a right to have the opportunity for your children to reach their greatest academic potential.

Your Responsibilities

Rights and responsibilities go hand in hand. As you may already know, and hopefully this book gave you additional information, there are many things you are expected to do to help your children be ready to learn and succeed in school. Here is a clear list that can work as a reminder.

- You are responsible for staying involved in the school.

- You are responsible for finding out what the school system is like in the U.S. and adapting to it as best as you can to help your children succeed.

- You are responsible for sending your children to school every day.

- You are responsible for making sure your children go to school well-rested, well-nourished, clean, and appropriately dressed.

- You are responsible for verifying that your children do their homework every day.

- You are responsible for providing a good environment at home that is conducive to studying and doing homework.

- You are responsible for limiting the time your children spend doing other activities besides schoolwork.

- You are responsible for providing a positive role model for your children.

- You are responsible for communicating with the school staff about anything you think it is important and keeping an open communication channel.

- You are responsible for attending parent/teacher conferences.

- You are responsible for not removing your children from school during the school year to take them on trips or to help at work.

- You are responsible for responding to school notices.

- You are responsible for notifying the school in writing if your children are absent due to sickness for up to three days. For longer absences, you need a doctor's note.

Cultural Tip

In addition to all the above responsibilities, you should learn English. This is the country you have chosen for yourself and your children; therefore, you have to make it a priority to learn the language. When you make an effort to learn English, once again you are setting an example. You are trying to assimilate to this culture, and that will be a key to your success. Think about this—you made a huge effort leaving your home country behind to come to the United States. Take full advantage of being here by learning English so all doors will be open to you.

A Final Note of Encouragement

I hope this book has helped you erase some of your fears and concerns as you journey through the American school system. The more information you have, the better the opportunities you will be able to offer your children. Remember that they deserve the best and that getting a seat in school is not enough. You have in your hands the chance to look for the best school, the best programs, and the best tools so they can achieve academic success. And the most important thing—your support is the fundamental key to opening the door to that success. Good luck!

About the Author

Mariela Dabbah was born in Buenos Aires, Argentina. She has a Masters' Degree in Philosophy and Literature from the University of Buenos Aires. She has lived in New York since 1988, where for twelve years she was the owner of a bilingual book distributor that served the public school system. She developed a Parent Involvement Division that provided parent and teacher training throughout the United States. One of her most exciting experiences was training Yup'ik parents and librarians in Bethel, Alaska.

Ms. Dabbah is the author of *Cómo Conseguir Trabajo en los Estados Unidos, Guía Especial para Latinos*, published by Sphinx Publishing, and of the book of short stories *Cuentos de Nuevos Aires y Buena York*, published by Metafrasta. Her book, *The Latino Advantage in the Workplace*, written with Arturo Poiré, was published in November 2006 by Sphinx Publishing.

Ms. Dabbah was invited to numerous TV and radio programs such as "Despierta América" on Univisión, "Cada día con María Antonietta" on Telemundo, "Directo desde Estados Unidos" on CNN en español, and "All Things Considered" on NPR, among others.

She lives in Westchester, New York. You can contact her through her email at mariela@marieladabbah.com or you can get more information about her books and speaking activities at **www.marieladabbah.com**.